Here Comes the Year

Eileen Spinelli · Keiko Narahashi

Henry Holt and Company · New York

I am the January dark,
dappled and deep,
teasing you, easing you
out of your cuddle-down sleep,
announcing it's morning,
having a bit of fun
staying up way past my bedtime,
replacing the sun.

I am the February frost
strumming the air,
etching feathery sketches of ice,
glistening everywhere,
zinging the tips of your fingers,
tinting your ears and your nose
redder than holly berries,
nipping your toes.

I am the March wind
prattling by,
pulling the last bit of winter
all through the sky,
knocking down icicles
with a tin-tin-tinkling sound,
setting old leaves to turn
like a merry-go-round.

I am the April rain,
a silvery spray
puddling streets and sidewalks,
splashing away,
a playful chorus of drip-drops
piping along—
tug on your boots and your raincoat,
maybe I'll teach you my song.

I am the May flowers,
sudden and sweet,
spattering giddy colors
up this road, down that street,
nodding in country gardens,
banking the river in drifts,
delivered in baskets and jam jars—
unexpected doorstep gifts.

I am the June sun,
dazzling, bold,
melting across the afternoon
in ripples of gold,
warming the cat's midday nap,
glazing the crowded beach,
waving lazy ribbons of flame
just out of reach.

I am the July thunderstorm
wild with glee,
crashing against the silence,
churning the sea,
spearing the clouds with lightning,
enjoying my game,
leaving rather abruptly—
just as I came.

I am the shooting stars of August—
Perseids so bright—
sparkling, spilling like diamonds
down through the night,
skittering-glittering cinders
springing a summer surprise,
spiraling toward your window,
amazing your eyes.

I am the September harvest,
honey from hives,
berries in patches and thickets,
meadow-grown chives,
apples from cool, scented orchards,
corn from bountiful farms,
ripened backyard tomatoes
that spill from your arms.

I am the October moon,
plump as you please,
teetering on rooftops,
leaping the trees,
shimmering, simmering orange,
tugging the ocean's tide,
inviting you to dance for me
before you run inside.

I am the November leaves
fluttering down,
a crunchy rumpus of shades and shapes
to carpet the town,
a gold and crimson flotilla
sailing the shallow brook,
a cozy basket of autumn
to press inside a book.

I am the December snow
hugging the hills,
roller-coastering merry sleds,
pillowing spills,
drifting onto the highway,
slowing the evening rush,
pulling a blanket over the earth,
dusting your dreams . . .

hush . . .

hush.